This Walker book belongs to:

_____

_____

withdrawn

First published 1991 in *Greek Myths*
by Walker Books Ltd, 87 Vauxhall Walk, London SE11 5HJ

This edition published 2017

2 4 6 8 10 9 7 5 3 1

© 1991, 2006, 2017 Marcia Williams

The right of Marcia Williams to be identified as author/illustrator of this work
has been asserted by her in accordance with the Copyright, Designs and Patents Act 1988

This book has been typeset in Goudy Old Style

Printed and bound in Great Britain by Clays Ltd, St Ives plc

British Library Cataloguing in Publication Data:
a catalogue record for this book is available from the British Library

ISBN 978-1-4063-7157-4

www.walker.co.uk

Theseus and the Minotaur
&
Arachne versus Athene

Marcia Williams

WALKER BOOKS
AND SUBSIDIARIES
LONDON · BOSTON · SYDNEY · AUCKLAND

Contents

Theseus and the Minotaur

Arachne versus Athene

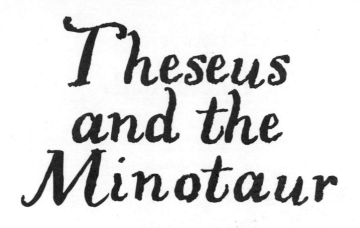

Theseus and the Minotaur

Chapter One
The Tribute

King Minos, who ruled over the Greek island
of Crete, was the son of the great god Zeus,
and a mighty ruler. King Minos hated the
people of Athens because he believed that
they had killed his son, Androgeus, after
he had won all the prizes at the Athenian
games. King Minos was heartbroken, for
he had loved his son dearly.

"I'd like to see them all dead!" King Minos roared and he gathered together a vast army to wage war against Athens.

The strength of this army, and the anger of King Minos, made King Aegeus of Athens fear for his people's safety. So to save Athens from destruction, King Aegeus agreed to a terrible, terrible tribute.

Every year, at the spring equinox, the Athenians were to send seven youths and

seven maidens across the sea to Crete, where they would be sacrificed to the man-eating Minotaur.

The Minotaur was a vast and powerful beast: half-man and half-bull – a truly terrifying creature. The labyrinth it lived in had been designed by the inventor and craftsman Daedalus, and was a miraculous maze of twists and turns. Once inside the labyrinth there was no escape and all who

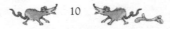

entered were destined to be devoured by
the savage, blood-thirsty Minotaur. It was
a terrible price to pay, even for the death
of a king's son.

King Aegeus of Athens had already sent
this cruel payment to King Minos twice –
and now the time had come again. There
was a great weeping and wailing throughout
Athens as lots were drawn to see who must
travel in the black-sailed ship to Crete.

"Bring them to the palace, so I can bid them farewell," ordered the king. "It is a terrible death, but I gave my oath and must keep it."

The following day, there was a knock on the palace door and in marched the soldiers with seven fine youths and seven beautiful maidens.

"Yes, you are all quite perfect," declared the king with a sigh.

"Father!" King Aegeus's son, Theseus, cried.

"How can you let these poor young people go? It is time we put an end to this cruelty. If you won't do it, I will go to Crete in the place of one of these poor sacrifices and kill the Minotaur myself!"

"Fat chance," wept the Minotaur's intended victims. "It is well known that nobody escapes from the labyrinth alive."

"They are quite right," said Theseus's horrified father. "You will never kill the

Minotaur! You won't be able to take a sword into the labyrinth and he is too strong, even for you. You will just end up as his next meal."

"No," cried Theseus, "I will go and I will kill him. I have killed monsters before and I'll kill this one. For the sake of all Athenians, I must do this."

King Aegeus begged his son not to go, but Theseus would not be dissuaded.

"Sorry, Dad, I have to," said Theseus, hugging his father.

"You really, really don't!" wept his father.

"Oh, but I do. The honour of Athens depends on it."

So Theseus set out for Crete, hoisting the black sail as a sign of respect for the young victims. He promised his father that he would return with a white sail, as a sign of his success.

"We will all return," he reassured his father. "Every one of us!"

"I will not sleep until you do," declared Aegeus, distraught. "I will stand guard on the cliff top waiting to see your white sail returning in triumph across the waves."

Chapter Two
Ariadne

Theseus and the other tributes sailed across
the Aegean Sea towards Crete. Great storms
battered the little ship and the passengers
were filled with fear. Only Theseus remained
cheerful, for his courage was such that he felt
invincible and was sure he could outwit the
sea, just as he planned to outwit the Minotaur.

Finally, the black-sailed ship landed on

the coast of Crete, where King Minos and his daughter Ariadne were waiting to greet the Minotaur's next feast. When Ariadne saw King Aegeus's handsome son Theseus amongst the tributes, she immediately fell madly in love with him.

She begged her father to spare his life, "Oh Father, look how handsome the young prince is. You cannot let him die such a terrible death."

But King Minos was unmoved. "If he

chooses to sacrifice himself to the Minotaur, so be it. Throw him into prison with the others," he ordered the guards, "and let him be the first one fed to the beast in the morning."

That night the Athenians were all locked in a dungeon close to the labyrinth. They lay huddled together, weeping and wailing as they listened to the hungry roar of the Minotaur. Only Theseus slept, seemingly undaunted by the terrible task ahead of him. Then, in the darkest hours of the night, he felt a hand on his shoulder. It was Ariadne, who had crept softly past the guards and let herself into the dungeon.

"Theseus," Ariadne whispered as she shook him awake. "If you promise to marry me,

you can have this sword to help you kill the
Minotaur and this ball of thread, which will
guide you out of the maze."

Theseus looked upon Ariadne and was so
overcome by her beauty, that even if she had
offered him neither sword nor ball of thread,
he would have agreed to marry her anyway.

"Of course I'll marry you," he promised,
"and we will sail back to Athens together in
triumph."

"Here then, hide these quickly," whispered

Ariadne. "I'll be waiting for you when you
have killed the beast."

Ariadne disappeared into the shadows and
Theseus hid the sword and the thread under
his clothes. Then he lay down again, trying
to sleep and not to think of what lay ahead
of him.

Chapter Three
The Minotaur

As the morning hours approached, Theseus's courage was sorely tested and he began to wonder if he would ever see his father again or behold the beauty of his wife-to-be, Ariadne. At the first light of dawn, the guards stirred themselves and unlocked the great door to the labyrinth. Theseus was the first to

enter and the other Athenians huddled close behind him. The door was slammed shut and they were left together in the gloom.

Theseus tried to reassure the poor sacrifices, but they were terrified. They stayed close to the locked door, crying most piteously. Theseus wasted no time – he tied one end of the thread to the bars on the door and set off with his sword in search of the Minotaur.

The labyrinth was even more confusing
than he had imagined, it was a maze of cold,
dark passages. Some led nowhere and Theseus
would find himself up against damp and slimy
walls, while others took him deeper into the
maze. All along the passageways, he held on

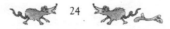

tightly to Ariadne's sword, even as the roar
of the Minotaur became louder and closer.

Theseus's heart began to beat wildly in his
chest. He could almost feel the beast's breath
upon him. Then, quite suddenly, he was
face-to-face with the hideous monster –
its eyes glowing red in the gloom. The
Minotaur was larger and more terrible than
Theseus had ever imagined, but it was too
late now – there was no escape. Gathering
all his courage, Theseus charged. The struggle

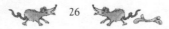

was long and fierce, for the Minotaur was
enormously strong, and it seemed certain
that Theseus would be its next meal. But
the Minotaur was caught off guard, for he
was not expecting to be attacked by someone
carrying a sword. Finally, Theseus drove the
sword through the Minotaur's heart and it
sank to the ground – dead.

Theseus followed the thread quickly back
through the confusing twists and turns of the
labyrinth until, with a huge sigh of relief, he

reached the entrance. The young Athenians
could hardly believe their eyes, for none had
dared to hope that Theseus would triumph.
A huge cheer rose from their midst as they re-
alized that they would live to see another day!

Chapter Four
The Wedding

Hearing the cheers of Theseus and his friends, Ariadne quickly unlocked the door.

"Hurry, I have drugged the guards, but we must go! We must be at sea before they wake," she cried.

Without another word, everyone ran for
the ship, quickly raised the sail and set their
course for Athens. After a few days at sea,
they stopped at an island so that Theseus and
Ariadne could be wed, just as Theseus had
promised. The wedding was a small but joyful
party, for everyone was delighted to celebrate
the union of their two saviours. After the
wedding, Ariadne lay down to rest in the
shade of a tree, while the others gathered

together enough provisions for the remainder
of the journey.

"Be quick," begged Theseus, "for we have
already been too long and my poor father will
be anxious."

The ship was loaded with fresh water and
the sweet fruit of the island and soon they
were ready to set sail again. Theseus went to
wake his new bride, but as he bent to kiss her,
he paused. He began to think of all the

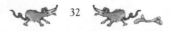

suffering her father had caused his family and so many other Athenian families. How could he possibly return to his father and his country married to the daughter of their worst enemy?

"Dad would never forgive me," he thought. "I have fulfilled my promise to her by marrying her. It wouldn't be fair to her to take her back to Athens where she would be hated and reviled. I should leave her here, sleeping happily."

So Theseus blew his sleeping bride a parting kiss and ran back to the ship. The Athenians hoisted the anchor and were a distant speck on the horizon when poor Ariadne awoke.

Chapter Five
The Homecoming

Meanwhile, King Aegeus watched anxiously for his son's ship to return.

"Theseus should be home by now," he muttered to himself each day, as he paced up and down along the cliffs. "He must be dead –

I told him not to go. Ah, but I mustn't give up hope, maybe he's alive. Yes, yes! There is still a chance. I must wait to see the colour of the sail. My heart may yet be filled with joy."

Unfortunately, all was not as it should have been, for in his haste to return to his father, Theseus had forgotten to change the ship's sail from black to white and, as the ship came into view, the first thing King Aegeus saw was the black sail! Theseus's father was overwhelmed with grief. Certain that his beloved son was

dead, he threw himself off the cliff, onto the rocks below, where the waves took his body and buried it in the ocean depths.

When Theseus's ship anchored, he was greeted with the terrible news. Poor Theseus, he was filled with sorrow and regret.

"How could I have been so thoughtless?" he wept and he mourned the death of his father.

As other parents celebrated their children's return, the whole of Athens hailed Theseus as a hero, and after the funeral of King Aegeus he was crowned the new king of Athens.

"I will try to be a great king in honour of my father," promised Theseus, "and the killing of the Minotaur will not be my last victory!"

Arachne versus Athene

Chapter One
The Boast

Arachne lived with her father in a poor village in the area of Greece known as Lydia. She was not a very beautiful girl, or a very nice one.

"This village is a dump!" she complained to her father. "I'm special; I should be living in a palace, you silly old man!"

"Yes, Petal," replied her father, who loved her in spite of her boastful ways and knew better than to argue with her.

Arachne was brilliant at weaving and never stopped boasting about her skill. She was probably better at weaving than anyone else in Greece but boy, did she know it! If you met her, she would certainly tell you this herself – many, many times. She never tired of telling

everyone just how amazing she was, which was why most of her neighbours had stopped visiting her!

"What I don't know about weaving just isn't worth knowing!" she bragged. "I'm the best! I'm the finest! I'm number one! Yes – me, me, me!"

 Although not many people actually liked Arachne, everyone did admit that she was indeed a very fine weaver. In fact, most people thought that her skill must have been learned from the great goddess, Athene. This was actually true, but arrogant Arachne denied it, believing that she was even better than the goddess.

"I know you all think that I learned my skill from Athene," Arachne shouted out of her window one day, "but it's rubbish. Athene couldn't even weave a nappy. Compared to me she's a total novice!"

Arachne's father pulled her back from the window and slammed the shutters closed. He begged her not to compare herself to Athene, for the gods were quick to anger, especially when humans claimed such great powers.

"Please don't compare yourself to Athene," he begged. "Please, please don't. If you anger Athene, there's no knowing what she might do."

But nothing could stop Arachne's conceited bragging and she issued a challenge to Athene – a weaving contest.

"Why don't you come down off your Mount, Athene, and prove that you're better than me?" she dared.

"You've really done it now, Arachne," gasped her father. "Nobody challenges the gods and lives to tell the tale."

Chapter Two
The Old Woman

The days passed and when nothing too awful happened to Arachne, her father began to hope that Athene might just have overlooked his daughter's arrogance. Then one day, there was a knock at their door and an ugly old woman, who he'd

never seen before, asked to see Arachne.

"What do you want, you old hag?" said
Arachne, with her usual lack of charm. "If
you want to see my brilliant weaving you've
no chance – you're far too dirty and smelly
to come inside."

"No, my dear," replied the old woman,
"I have not come to see your weaving, but
to beg you to withdraw your challenge to
Athene."

"And why should I?" demanded Arachne. "I'm much better than her and she knows it. What's more, it's none of your business!"

"I think if you apologize very, very quickly, she will forgive you for being so foolish, my dear," persisted the old woman.

Arachne laughed and declared that she could out-weave anyone – even a goddess.

"My challenge to Athene stands. I am the best and not just the best but the most outstanding best!"

At this the old woman quivered from head to toe with rage, so much so that her rags began to fall away. Then quite suddenly, the

old hag was transformed into her true self –
the all-powerful goddess, Athene.

"Don't you know who I am?" bellowed the
goddess, quite beside herself with anger.

"Oh yes, you're Athene!" replied Arachne,
without any surprise. "But I'm not afraid of
you!"

"Well, you
should be, my
dear," whispered
the goddess.

Chapter Three
The Challenge

Athene had given Arachne every chance, but now she decided it was time to teach her a lesson, so she accepted the foolish girl's challenge. Two looms were set up, side by side. The finest threads were fetched from Mount Olympus and the contest began.

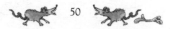

"Ready?" asked Athene.

"Ready!" replied Arachne.

All day the shuttles flashed back and
forth, weaving designs in an astonishing
variety of colours and hues. Athene's cloth
was perfection and depicted the gods of
Mount Olympus in all their glory. While
Arachne's cloth was also perfection, it showed
the gods as silly, drunken fools. When the sun

went down and the last threads had been woven, the contest ended.

"Phew!" sighed Arachne. "I'm glad that's over."

"Gods never get tired," replied Athene.

Athene then turned to look at Arachne's work.

"Admit it – it's better than yours," said

Arachne, still not realizing the danger she was in.

Athene stared at the work in amazement – it was quite perfect ... almost as perfect as her own. The weave was even throughout and the design most intricate and wonderfully executed.

"There must be a fault in it somewhere, she's only mortal," thought Athene, peering closer at the design.

Stepping back, Athene suddenly saw how
Arachne's design insulted the gods and she
exploded with rage! Arachne had gone too far.
Boasting was one thing, but depicting the gods
as drunken fools was intolerable. Taking up her
shuttle, she slashed Arachne's cloth in two.

"You're just jealous," laughed Arachne.

At this, Athene turned on Arachne and beat her about the head with the shuttle, chasing her around and around the room. Arachne had never seen such fury and finally understood how much trouble she was in. She tried to defend herself, but she was no match for the angry goddess. Fearful of what the goddess might do next, Arachne grabbed hold of a rope. She quickly tied a noose

around her neck and hung herself from a beam! Arachne swayed back and forth on the rope as the life was slowly squeezed out of her.

"Not before time," snarled Athene. "There'll be no more weaving for you!"

Chapter Four
The Reprieve

Hearing the commotion Arachne's father rushed into the room and saw his daughter hanging on the end of the rope.

"Oh, my poor daughter!" he cried, horrified at her plight.

He turned to Athene and begged her to spare his daughter's life. "Please let her live, oh great and powerful Athene," he cried.

"Give me one good reason," snapped the goddess.

There was silence.

"Not so easy, is it?" laughed the goddess.

"Well, she is my one and only daughter," Arachne's father finally replied, "and I do love her."

Very grudgingly, the goddess agreed to let
Arachne live. She sprinkled herbs all over
Arachne's still-dangling body as her father
sighed with relief. But quickly his relief
turned to horror as he watched a dreadful
transformation start to take place…

First, Arachne's hair fell out. "Not my
beautiful coiffure!" she cried.

Then her nose, ears and legs fell off. "I am

not the person I was," she wailed.

Next her arms disappeared, so that her fingers cleaved to her sides. "This is not good, Athene. What are you doing to me? Oh, father, you should have let me die!"

As poor Arachne cried out in vain, her head and body began to shrink, until she was no bigger than a fist. "Daddy, can you still hear me?" she squeaked.

Finally, the rope by which Arachne was dangling became a fine, silken thread.

"I warned you not to anger the gods," laughed Athene. "Now you can weave all you want and boast all you want, because nobody will ever hear you."

Athene had taken her revenge – she had turned Arachne into a spider!

"There's weaving ... and there's weaving

webs…" sobbed Arachne. But nobody, not even her father, could hear her.

Other fabulous retellings by
Marcia Williams

978-1-4063-6279-4

978-1-4063-6272-5

978-1-4063-6276-3

978-1-4063-6273-2

978-1-4063-5694-6

978-1-4063-5695-3

978-1-4063-5693-9

978-1-4063-5692-2

Available from all good booksellers

www.walker.co.uk